WHAT'S COOKING?

THAI

PARRAGON

First published in Great Britain in 1997 by
Parragon
Unit 13–17
Avonbridge Trading Estate
Atlantic Road
Avonmouth
Bristol BS11 9QD

ISBN: 0-7525-2251-5

Produced by Haldane Mason, London

Acknowledgements
Art Director: Ron Samuels
Editors: Jo-Anne Cox, Charles Dixon-Spain
Design: Errol Campbell
Photography: Sue Atkinson, Iain Bagwell,
Martin Brigdale, Karl Adamson

Printed in Italy

Material in this book has previously appeared in
Thai Cooking by Carol Bowen, *Thai Side Dishes* by
Sue Ashworth and *Vegetarian Thai Cooking* by
Cara Hobday

Note
Cup measurements in this book are for
American cups. Tablespoons are assumed to be
15ml. Unless otherwise stated, milk is assumed to
be full fat, eggs are standard size 3 and pepper is
freshly ground black pepper.

CONTENTS

Introduction

Thai cooking is renowned for its fragrant spices, aromatic herbs, exotic fruits and vegetables, a wide range of rice and noodle dishes, and flavours that range from mild to hot and spicy. Many of the dishes are stir-fried, so they are not only excitingly different, but also quick and easy to do.

Any well-equipped Western kitchen will be fine for cooking Thai food, but if you intend to cook such food regularly, then you will find a wok most useful, as it is ideal for braising, steaming and deep-frying, as well as the usual stir-frying. A pestle and mortar is a must for grinding up spices and seeds, and a bamboo steamer (which can be used in conjunction with a wok) produces vegetables with a delicate flavour and crunchy texture.

Thai cuisine uses several special ingredients, almost all of which will be available at the supermarket. Bean sprouts, chillies, coconut, coriander, galangal, ginger root and lemon grass are all available dried, but are best used fresh. Similarly, your dishes will benefit from the freshest vegetables, meats and fish, because the colours, tastes and aromas will be all the more striking.

Like many oriental cuisines, Thai cooking places great emphasis on fresh vegetables and fruits, rice and noodle dishes, and the inventive use of endless combinations of herbs, spices and seasonings to give the food its characteristic Thai flavour. From Red Curry Fishcakes and Little Golden Parcels to fluffy Thai Jasmine Rice, Duck with Ginger & Lime and Mangoes with Sticky Rice, this book is the perfect introduction to the best of Thai cooking. Each dish is photographed in full colour, so you can see exactly how delicious these recipes are.

Red Curry Fish Cakes

Thai fishcakes make a tasty starter and good introduction to a Thai-style meal.

SERVES 4–6

1 kg/2 lb fish fillets or prepared seafood, such as cod, haddock, prawns (shrimp), crab meat or lobster
1 egg, beaten • 2 tbsp chopped fresh coriander
Red Curry Paste (see page 24)
1 bunch spring onions (scallions), finely chopped
vegetable oil, for deep-frying • chilli flowers

Cucumber salad:
1 large cucumber, peeled and grated
2 shallots, peeled and grated
2 red chillies, deseeded and very finely chopped
2 tbsp fish sauce • 2 tbsp dried powdered shrimps
1½–2 tbsp lime juice

1 Place the fish in a blender or food processor with the egg, coriander and curry paste and purée until smooth and well blended. Turn the mixture into a bowl, add the spring onions (scallions) and mix well to combine.

2 Taking 2 tablespoons of the fish mixture at a time, shape into balls, then flatten them slightly with your fingers to make fishcakes.

3 Heat the oil in a wok or pan until hot, add a few of the fishcakes and deep-fry for 2–3 minutes until brown and cooked through. Remove with a slotted spoon and drain on paper towels. Keep warm while cooking the remaining fishcakes.

4 Meanwhile, to make the cucumber salad, mix the cucumber with the shallots, chillies, fish sauce, dried shrimps and lime juice.

5 Serve the warm fishcakes with cucumber salad.

Pork & Prawn (Shrimp) Sesame Toasts

This classic Thai snack is a great nibble for serving at parties.

SERVES 4

250 g/ 8 oz lean pork
250 g/ 8 oz/²⁄₃ cup uncooked peeled prawns (shrimp), deveined
4 spring onions (scallions), trimmed • 1 garlic clove, crushed
1 tbsp chopped fresh coriander (cilantro) leaves and stems
1 tbsp fish sauce • 1 egg
8–10 slices of thick-cut white bread
3 tbsp sesame seeds • 150 ml/¼ pint/²⁄₃ cup vegetable oil
salt and pepper

To garnish:
sprigs of fresh coriander (cilantro)
red (bell) pepper, sliced finely

1 Put the pork, prawns (shrimp), spring onions (scallions), garlic, coriander (cilantro), fish sauce, egg and seasoning into a food processor or blender. Process for a few seconds to chop the ingredients finely. Transfer the mixture to a bowl. Alternatively, chop the pork, prawns (shrimp) and spring onions (scallions) very finely, and mix with the garlic, coriander (cilantro), fish sauce, beaten egg and seasoning until well combined.

2 Spread the pork and prawn (shrimp) mixture thickly over the bread so that it reaches to the edges. Cut off the crusts and cut each slice of bread into 4 pieces. Sprinkle the topping liberally with sesame seeds.

3 Heat the oil in a wok or frying pan (skillet). Fry a few pieces of the bread, topping side down first so that it sets the egg, for about 2 minutes or until golden brown. Turn the pieces over

and cook the other side for about 1 minute. Remove the pork and prawn (shrimp) toasts with a slotted spoon and drain them on paper towels. Fry the remaining pieces in batches until they are all cooked.

4 Serve garnished with sprigs of fresh coriander (cilantro) and (bell) pepper.

Aubergine (Eggplant) Dipping Platter

Dipping platters are a very sociable dish, bringing together all the diners at the table. This substantial dip is served with vegetables as an appetizer.

SERVES 4

1 aubergine (eggplant), peeled and cut into 2.5 cm/1 inch cubes
3 tbsp sesame seeds, roasted in a dry pan over a low heat
1 tsp sesame oil
grated rind and juice of ½ lime
1 small shallot, diced
½ tsp salt • 1 tsp sugar
1 red chilli, deseeded and sliced • pepper

To serve:
125 g/4 oz broccoli florets • 2 carrots, cut into matchsticks
125 g/4 oz/8 baby sweetcorn cobs, cut in half lengthways
2 celery stalks, cut into matchsticks
1 baby red cabbage, cut into 8 wedges, the leaves of each wedge held together by the core

1 Cook the diced aubergine (eggplant) in boiling water for 7–8 minutes.

2 Meanwhile, grind the sesame seeds with the oil in a food processor or pestle and mortar.

3 Add the aubergine (eggplant), lime rind and juice, shallot, salt, sugar and chilli in that order to the sesame seeds. Process, or chop and mash by hand, until smooth.

4 Adjust the seasoning if necessary then spoon into a bowl. Serve surrounded by the broccoli, carrots, sweetcorn cobs, celery and cabbage.

Little Golden Parcels

These simply prepared little parcels will draw admiring gasps from your guests.

MAKES 30

1 garlic clove, crushed
1 tsp chopped coriander (cilantro) root • 1 tsp pepper
250 g / 8 oz boiled mashed potato
175 g / 6 oz / 1 cup water chestnuts, chopped finely
1 tsp grated ginger root • 2 tbsp ground roast peanuts
2 tsp light soy sauce • ½ tsp salt
½ tsp sugar • 30 wonton sheets, defrosted
1 tsp cornflour (cornstarch), made into a paste
with 1 tbsp cold water
vegetable oil, for deep-frying • fresh chives, to garnish
sweet chilli sauce, to serve

1 Combine all the ingredients thoroughly, except the wonton sheets, cornflour (cornstarch) paste and oil.

2 Lay 4 wonton sheets out on a work surface (counter), keeping the remaining sheets covered with a damp cloth. Put a teaspoonful of the mixture on each wonton sheet. Drizzle a line of the cornflour (cornstarch) paste around each sheet, about 1 cm/½ inch from the edges.

3 Bring all 4 corners to the centre of each sheet and press together to form a little bags. Continue the process of filling and wrapping until all the wonton sheets are used.

4 Meanwhile, heat 5 cm/ 2 inches of the vegetable oil in a deep saucepan until a light haze appears on top. Lower in the parcels, in batches of 3. Fry until golden brown, then remove with a slotted spoon and leave to drain on paper towels.

5 Tie a chive around the neck of each bag to garnish, and serve with a sweet chilli sauce for dipping.

Sweetcorn Patties

These are a delicious addition to any party buffet, and very simple to prepare. Serve with a sweet chilli sauce.

SERVES 12

325 g / 11 oz can of sweetcorn, drained
1 onion, chopped finely
1 tsp curry powder
1 garlic clove, crushed
1 tsp ground coriander
2 spring onions (scallions), sliced
3 tbsp plain (all-purpose) flour
½ tsp baking powder
salt
1 large egg
4 tbsp sunflower oil

1 Mash the drained sweetcorn lightly in a medium-sized bowl. Add all the remaining ingredients, except for the sunflower oil, one at a time, stirring after each addition.

2 Heat the oil in a frying pan (skillet). Drop tablespoonfuls of the mixture carefully on to the hot oil, far enough apart for them not to run into each other as they cook.

3 Cook for 4–5 minutes, turning each patty once, until they are golden brown and firm. Take care not to turn them too soon, or they will break up in the pan.

4 Remove from the pan with a spatula or fish slice and drain on paper towels. Serve quickly while still warm.

Fish with Ginger Butter

Whole mackerel or trout are stuffed with herbs, wrapped in foil or banana leaves, baked and drizzled with a ginger butter.

SERVES 4

4 x 250 g/8 oz whole trout or mackerel, gutted
4 tbsp chopped fresh coriander (cilantro)
5 garlic cloves, crushed
2 tsp grated lemon or lime zest
2 tsp vegetable oil
banana leaves, for wrapping (optional)
90 g/3 oz/6 tbsp butter
1 tbsp grated ginger root
1 tbsp light soy sauce • salt and pepper

To garnish:
sprigs of fresh coriander (cilantro)
lemon or lime wedges

1 Wash and dry the fish. Mix the coriander (cilantro) with the garlic, lemon or lime zest and salt and pepper to taste. Spoon into the fish cavities. Brush each fish with a little oil and season well with salt and pepper.

2 Place each fish on a double thickness of baking parchment or foil and wrap up well to enclose. Alternatively, wrap in banana leaves. Place on a baking sheet and bake in a preheated oven at 190°C/375°F/Gas Mark 5 for about 25 minutes or until the flesh will flake easily.

3 Meanwhile, melt the butter in a small pan. Add the grated ginger and stir until well mixed, then stir in the soy sauce.

4 To serve, unwrap the fish parcels, drizzle over the ginger butter and garnish with coriander (cilantro) and lemon or lime wedges.

Bamboo Shoots with Cucumber

This simple side dish is the perfect accompaniment to a Thai main meal. Salting the cucumber before it is stir-fried draws out the moisture so that it stays crisp.

SERVES 4

½ cucumber • 2 tbsp sesame oil
4 shallots, chopped finely • 1 garlic clove, sliced finely
350 g/12 oz can of bamboo shoots, drained
1 tbsp dry sherry • 1 tbsp soy sauce
2 tsp cornflour (cornstarch) • 1 tsp sesame seeds • salt

To garnish:
2 red chilli flowers • sliced spring onions (scallions)

1 Slice the cucumber thinly and sprinkle with salt. Leave for 10–15 minutes, then rinse with cold water. Meanwhile, to make chilli flowers for garnishing, hold the stem of the chilli and cut down its length several times with a sharp knife. Place in a bowl of chilled water until the 'petals' turn out. Remove the chilli seeds when the 'petals' have opened.

2 Heat the sesame oil in a wok or frying pan (skillet) and add the shallots and garlic. Stir-fry for 2 minutes, until golden. Add the bamboo shoots and cucumber and stir-fry for 2–3 minutes.

3 Blend together the sherry, soy sauce and cornflour (cornstarch). Add to the bamboo shoots and cucumber, stirring to combine. Cook for 1–2 minutes to thicken slightly, then add the sesame seeds and stir them through.

4 Transfer the vegetables to a warmed serving dish. Garnish with the chilli flowers and sliced spring onions (scallions). Serve at once.

Thai-Style Bananas

The Thais rarely finish a meal with an elaborate dessert, preferring a selection of tropical fruits. This is one of the mouth-watering exceptions.

SERVES 6

3 tbsp shredded fresh coconut
60 g/ 2 oz/ 4 tbsp unsalted butter
1 tbsp grated ginger root
grated zest of 1 orange
6 bananas
6 tbsp orange liqueur (Cointreau or Grand Marnier, for example)
3 tsp toasted sesame seeds
lime slices, to decorate
ice-cream, to serve (optional)

1 Heat a small non-stick frying pan (skillet) until hot. Add the coconut and cook, stirring, for about 1 minute until lightly coloured. Remove from the pan and allow to cool.

2 Heat the butter in a large frying pan (skillet) until it melts. Add the ginger and orange zest and mix well.

3 Peel and slice the bananas lengthways (and halve if they are very large). Place the bananas cut-side down in the butter mixture and cook for 1–2 minutes or until the sauce mixture starts to become sticky. Turn to coat in the sauce. Remove the bananas from the pan and place on warmed serving plates. Keep warm.

4 Return the pan to the heat and add the orange liqueur, stirring well to blend. Ignite with a taper, allow the flames to die down, then pour the liquid over the bananas.

5 Sprinkle with the coconut and sesame seeds and serve at once, decorated with slices of lime.

Baked Coconut Rice Pudding

A wonderful baked rice pudding cooked with flavoursome coconut milk and a little lime rind. Serve hot or chilled with fresh or stewed fruit.

SERVES 4

90 g/3 oz/scant ⅓ cup short or round-grain pudding rice
600 ml/1 pint/2½ cups coconut milk
300 ml/½ pint/1¼ cups milk
1 large strip lime rind
60 g/2 oz/⅓ cup caster sugar
knob of butter
pinch of ground star anise (optional)
fresh or stewed fruit, to serve

1 Heat the oven to 160°C/325°F/Gas Mark 2. Mix the rice with the coconut milk, milk, lime rind and sugar.

2 Pour the rice mixture into a lightly-greased 1.5 litre/2½ pint shallow ovenproof dish and dot the surface with a little butter. Bake in a preheated oven at 160°C/325°F/Gas Mark 3 for about 30 minutes.

3 Remove and discard the strip of lime. Stir the pudding well, add a pinch of ground star anise, if using, return to the oven and cook for 1–2 hours or until almost all the milk has been absorbed and a golden brown skin has formed on the top of the pudding. (Cover the top of the pudding with foil if it starts to brown too much towards the end of the cooking time.)

4 Serve the pudding warm or chilled with fresh or stewed fruit.

Pancakes Polamai

**These Thai pancakes are filled with an
exotic array of tropical fruits.**

SERVES 4

*125 g/ 4 oz/ 1 cup plain flour • pinch of salt • 1 egg
1 egg yolk • 300 ml/ ½ pint/ 1¼ cups coconut milk
4 tsp vegetable oil, plus oil for frying
flowers or sprigs of mint, to decorate*

Filling:

*1 banana • 1 paw-paw (papaya) • juice of 1 lime
2 passion fruit • 1 mango, peeled, stoned and sliced
4 lychees, stoned and halved • 1–2 tbsp honey*

1 To make the batter, sift the flour into a bowl with the salt. Make a well in the centre, add the egg and yolk and a little coconut milk. Gradually draw the flour into the egg mixture, beating well and gradually adding the remaining coconut milk to make a smooth batter. Add the oil and mix well. Cover and chill for 30 minutes.

2 To make the filling, peel and slice the banana and put in a bowl. Peel and slice the paw-paw (papaya), remove the seeds then cut into bite-sized chunks. Add to the banana with the lime juice and mix to coat.

3 Cut the passion fruit in half, scoop out the flesh and seeds and add to the banana mixture. Add the mango, lychees and honey and mix.

4 To make the pancakes, heat a little oil in a 15 cm/6 inch crêpe or frying pan (skillet). Pour in enough of the pancake batter to cover the base of the pan and tilt it so that it spreads thinly and evenly. Cook until the pancake is just set and the underside is lightly browned, turn and briefly cook the other side. Remove from the pan and keep warm. Repeat to make a total of 8 pancakes.

5 To serve, place a little of the prepared fruit filling along the centre of each pancake and, using both hands, roll it into a cone shape. Lay the pancakes seam-side down on warmed serving plates, allowing 2 pancakes per serving. Serve at once, decorated with flowers and mint sprigs, if liked.

Mangoes with Sticky Rice

This traditional South-east Asian dessert has to be included in this book, as every Thai cook knows how to make it, and it will round off any Thai meal perfectly.

SERVES 4

125 g / 4 oz / 1 cup glutinous (sticky) rice or short-grain pudding rice
250 ml / 8 fl oz / 1 cup coconut milk
60 g / 2 oz / 1/3 cup light muscovado sugar
1/2 tsp salt • 1 tsp sesame seeds, toasted
4 ripe mangoes, peeled, halved, stoned (pitted) and sliced

1 Put the rice into a colander and rinse well with plenty of cold water until the water runs clear. Transfer the rice to a large bowl, cover with cold water and leave to soak overnight, or for at least 12 hours. Drain well.

2 Line a bamboo basket or steamer with muslin (cheesecloth) or finely woven cotton cloth. Add the rice and steam over a pan of gently simmering water until the rice is tender, about 40 minutes. Remove from the heat and transfer the rice to a bowl.

3 Reserve 4 tablespoons of the coconut milk and put the remainder into a small saucepan with the sugar and salt. Heat and simmer gently for about 8 minutes until reduced by about one third.

4 Pour the coconut milk mixture over the rice, fluffing up the rice so that the mixture is absorbed. Set aside for 10–15 minutes.

5 Pack the rice into individual moulds and then invert them on to serving plates. Spoon a little reserved coconut milk over each mound and sprinkle with the sesame seeds. Arrange the sliced mango on the plates and serve, decorated with pieces of mango cut into shapes with tiny cutters.

Index

Thai Jasmine Rice

Every Thai meal has as its centrepiece a big bowl of steaming, fluffy Thai jasmine rice. The method used for cooking rice in Thailand is the absorption method, but the open pan method is also given below, as this is the one most familiar to Western cooks. Salt should not be added.

SERVES 3–4

Open pan method:
250 g/ 8 oz/ 1¼ cups Thai jasmine rice
1 litre/ 1¾ pints water

1 Rinse the rice in a sieve (strainer) under cold running water and leave to drain thoroughly.

2 Bring the water to the boil. Add the rice, stir and cook over a medium heat, uncovered, for 8–10 minutes.

3 Drain the rice and fork through lightly before serving.

Absorption method:
250 g/ 8 oz/ 1¼ cups Thai jasmine rice
450 ml/ ¾ pint water

1 Rinse the rice in a sieve (strainer) under cold running water.

2 Put the rice and water into a saucepan and bring to the boil. Stir once and then cover the pan tightly with the pan lid or a piece of foil. Lower the heat as much as possible and cook for 10 minutes. Leave to rest for 5 minutes, then fork through lightly and serve hot.

King Prawns (Jumbo Shrimp) in Red Curry Sauce

This inspired dish of prawns (shrimp) in a wonderfully spicy sauce is quick and simple, and will set your tasebuds alight!

SERVES 4

1 tbsp vegetable oil
6 spring onions (scallions), trimmed and sliced
1 stalk lemon grass
1 cm / ½ inch piece of fresh ginger root
250 ml / 8 fl oz / 1 cup coconut milk
2 tbsp Red Curry Paste (page 24)
1 tbsp fish sauce
500 g / 1 lb uncooked king prawns (jumbo shrimp)
1 tbsp chopped fresh coriander (cilantro)
fresh chillies, to garnish

1 Heat the vegetable oil in a wok or large frying pan (skillet) and fry the spring onions (scallions) gently until softened, about 2 minutes.

2 Bruise the stalk of lemon grass using a meat mallet or rolling pin. Peel and finely grate the piece of fresh ginger root. Add the bruised lemon grass and grated ginger root to the wok or frying pan (skillet) with the coconut milk, red curry paste and fish sauce. Heat until almost boiling.

3 Peel the prawns (shrimp), leaving the tails intact. Remove the black vein running down the back of each prawn (shrimp). Add the prawns (shrimp) to the wok or frying pan (skillet) with the chopped coriander (cilantro) and cook gently for 5 minutes. Serve the prawns (shrimp) with the red curry sauce, garnished with fresh chillies.

Kaffir Lime Mussels with Lemon Grass

Fresh mussels with a Far Eastern flavour.

SERVES 4

750 g/ 1½ lb live mussels • 1 tbsp sesame oil
3 shallots, chopped finely • 2 garlic cloves, chopped finely
1 stalk lemon grass • 2 kaffir lime leaves
2 tbsp chopped fresh coriander (cilantro)
finely grated rind of 1 lime • 2 tbsp lime juice
300 ml/ ½ pint/ 1¼ cups hot vegetable stock
crusty bread to serve

To garnish:
sprigs of fresh coriander (cilantro) • lime wedges

1 Scrub the mussels well under cold running water, removing the 'beards'. Keep rinsing until there is no trace of sand. Discard any that are damaged or remain open when tapped.

2 Heat the sesame oil in a large saucepan and fry the shallots and garlic gently until softened, about 2 minutes. Bruise the lemon grass, using a meat mallet or rolling pin, and add to the saucepan with the Kaffir lime leaves, coriander (cilantro), lime rind and juice, mussels and stock. Put the lid on the saucepan and cook over a medium heat for 3–5 minutes. Shake the saucepan occasionally.

3 Check that the mussels have opened and discard any that remain closed. Lift them out and transfer to 4 warmed soup plates. Boil the remaining liquid rapidly so that it reduces slightly. Remove the lemon grass and kaffir lime leaves, then pour the liquid over the mussels.

4 Garnish with the fresh coriander (cilantro) and lime wedges, and serve with chunks of crusty bread.

Shrimp Rolls

Tasty spring rolls made with shrimps.

SERVES 4

2 tbsp vegetable oil • 3 shallots, chopped very finely
1 carrot, cut into matchsticks
7 cm/3 inch piece of cucumber, cut into matchsticks
60 g/2 oz/½ cup bamboo shoots, shredded finely
125 g/4 oz/½ cup peeled (small) shrimps
90 g/3 oz/½ cup cooked long-grain rice
1 tbsp fish sauce or light soy sauce • 1 tsp sugar
2 tsp cornflour (cornstarch), blended in 2 tbsp cold water
8 × 25 cm/10 inch spring roll wrappers
oil for deep-frying • salt and pepper
Thai plum sauce, to serve

To garnish:
spring onions (scallions) • sprigs of fresh coriander (cilantro)

1 Heat the oil in a wok or frying pan (skillet) and add the shallots, carrot, cucumber and bamboo shoots. Stir-fry briskly for 2–3 minutes. Add the shrimps and rice, and cook for 2 minutes and season.

2 Mix together the fish sauce or soy sauce, sugar and blended cornflour (cornstarch). Add to the stir-fry and cook, stirring constantly, for about 1 minute, until thickened. Leave to cool slightly.

3 Place spoonfuls of the shrimp and vegetable mixture on the spring roll wrappers. Dampen the edges, fold in and roll them up to enclose the filling completely.

4 Heat the oil to 180–190°C/350–375°F or until a cube of bread browns in 30 seconds. Deep-fry the rolls until crisp and drain.

5 Serve garnished with spring onions (scallions) and coriander (cilantro) and accompanied by plum sauce.

Red Chicken Curry

The curry paste is fiery hot – for a milder version, reduce the number of chillies used.

SERVES 6

4 tbsp vegetable oil • 2 garlic cloves, crushed
400 ml/14 fl oz/1¾ cups coconut milk
6 chicken breast fillets, skinned and cut into bite-sized pieces
125 ml/4 fl oz/½ cup chicken stock • 2 tbsp fish sauce
3 tbsp thick coconut milk or cream
finely chopped chillies, lemon grass and lemon slices, to garnish
cooked rice, to serve

Red curry paste:
8 dried red chillies, deseeded and chopped
2.5 cm/1 inch piece of galangal or ginger root, peeled and sliced
3 stalks lemon grass, chopped • 1 garlic clove, peeled
2 tsp shrimp paste • 1 kaffir lime leaf, chopped
1 tsp ground coriander (cilantro) • ¾ tsp ground cumin
1 tbsp chopped fresh coriander • 1 tsp salt • 1 tsp black pepper

1 To make the curry paste, put all the ingredients in a food processor or blender and process until smooth.

2 Heat the oil in a large, heavy-based pan or wok. Add the garlic and cook for 1 minute or until golden. Stir in the curry paste and cook for 10–15 seconds then gradually add the coconut milk, stirring constantly (don't worry if the mixture starts to look curdled at this stage).

Add the chicken pieces and turn in the sauce mixture to coat. Cook gently for about 3–5 minutes or until almost tender. Stir in the chicken stock and fish sauce, mixing well, then cook for 2 minutes.

3 Transfer the chicken to a warmed dish. To serve, spoon on a little of the thick coconut milk or cream and garnish with chopped chillies, lemon grass and lemon slices. Serve with rice.

Green Chilli Chicken

**The chilli paste gives a hot, spicy flavour
and vibrant green colour to the chicken.**

SERVES 4

5 tbsp vegetable oil
500 g/ 1 lb boneless chicken breasts, sliced into thin strips
50 ml/ 2 fl oz/ ¼ cup coconut milk • 3 tbsp brown sugar
3 tsp fish sauce • 3 tbsp sliced red and green chillies, deseeded
4–6 tbsp chopped fresh basil
Kaffir lime leaves, sliced red chillies and chopped coriander
(cilantro), to garnish

Green curry paste:
2 tsp ground ginger • 2 tsp ground coriander
2 tsp caraway seeds • 2 tsp ground nutmeg
2 tsp shrimp paste • 2 tsp salt
2 tsp black pepper • pinch of ground cloves
1 stalk lemon grass, finely chopped
2 tbsp chopped coriander • 2 garlic cloves, peeled

1 To make the curry paste, place all the ingredients and 2 tablespoons of the oil in a food processor or blender and process to a smooth paste.

2 Heat the remaining oil in a heavy-based pan or wok. Add the curry paste and cook for about 30 seconds. Add the chicken strips to the wok and stir-fry over a high heat for about 2–3 minutes.

Add the coconut milk, brown sugar, fish sauce and chillies. Cook for 5 minutes, stirring.

3 Remove from the heat, add the basil and toss well to mix.

4 Transfer the chicken to a warmed serving dish and garnish with lime leaves, sliced red chillies and chopped coriander (cilantro). Serve with rice.

Peanut Sesame Chicken

A quick to make chicken and vegetable dish. Sesame and peanuts give it crunch and the fruit juice glaze gives a lovely shiny coating to the sauce.

SERVES 4

2 tbsp vegetable oil
2 tbsp sesame oil
500 g/ 1 lb boned and skinned chicken breasts, sliced into strips
250 g/ 8 oz broccoli, divided into small florets
250 g/ 8 oz baby sweetcorn cobs
1 small red (bell) pepper, cored, deseeded and sliced
2 tbsp soy sauce
250 ml/ 8 fl oz/ 1 cup orange juice
2 tsp cornflour (cornstarch)
2 tbsp toasted sesame seeds
60 g/ 2 oz/ ⅓ cup roasted, shelled, unsalted peanuts
rice or noodles, to serve

1 Heat the oils in a large, heavy-based frying pan (skillet) or wok, add the chicken strips and stir-fry until browned, about 4–5 minutes.

2 Add the broccoli, sweetcorn cobs and red (bell) pepper and stir-fry for 1–2 minutes.

3 Meanwhile, mix the soy sauce with the orange juice and cornflour (cornstarch). Stir into the chicken and vegetable mixture, stirring constantly until the sauce has slightly thickened and a glaze develops.

4 Stir in the sesame seeds and peanuts, mixing well. Heat for 3–4 minutes. Serve at once, with rice or noodles.

Duck with Ginger & Lime

**Just the thing for a lazy summer day –
slices of roasted duck breasts on a bed of
assorted fresh salad leaves.**

SERVES 6

*3 boneless Barbary duck breasts, about 250 g/ 8 oz each
salt • assorted salad leaves, to serve*

Dressing:

*125 ml/ 4 fl oz/ ½ cup olive oil • 2 tsp sesame oil
2 tbsp lime juice • grated rind and juice of 1 orange
2 tsp Thai fish sauce • 1 tbsp grated ginger root
1 garlic clove, crushed • 2 tsp light soy sauce
3 spring onions (scallions), finely chopped • 1 tsp sugar*

1 Wash the duck breasts, dry on paper towels, then cut in half. Prick the skin all over with a fork and season well with salt.

2 Place the duck pieces, skin-side down, on a wire rack or trivet over a roasting tin (pan). Cook the duck in a preheated oven at 200°C/ 400°F/Gas Mark 6 for 10 minutes.

3 Turn the duck pieces over and cook for 12–15 minutes, or until the duck is cooked, but still pink in the centre, and the skin is crisp.

4 To make the dressing, beat the oils with the lime juice, orange rind and juice, fish sauce, ginger, garlic, soy sauce, spring onions (scallions) and sugar until well blended.

5 Remove the duck from the oven, allow to cool, then cut into thick slices. Add a little dressing to moisten and coat the duck.

6 To serve, arrange the salad leaves on a serving dish. Top with the sliced duck breasts and drizzle with the remaining dressing. Serve at once.

Peppered Beef Cashew

A simple but stunning dish of tender strips of beef mixed with vegetables and crunchy cashew nuts, coated in a hot sauce. Serve with rice noodles.

SERVES 4

1 tbsp groundnut or sunflower oil
1 tbsp sesame oil
1 onion, sliced
1 garlic clove, crushed
1 tbsp grated ginger root
500 g/ 1 lb fillet or rump steak, cut into thin strips
2 tsp palm sugar or demerara sugar
2 tbsp light soy sauce
1 small yellow (bell) pepper, cored, deseeded and sliced
1 red (bell) pepper, cored, deseeded and sliced
4 spring onions (scallions), chopped
2 celery stalks, chopped
4 large open-cap mushrooms, sliced
4 tbsp roasted cashew nuts
3 tbsp stock or white wine
rice noodles, to serve

1 Heat the oils in a wok or large, heavy-based frying pan (skillet). Add the onion, garlic and ginger, and stir-fry for about 2 minutes until softened and lightly coloured.

2 Add the steak strips and stir-fry for 2–3 minutes, until the meat has browned. Add the sugar and soy sauce, mixing well.

3 Add the (bell) peppers, spring onions (scallions), celery, mushrooms and cashews, mixing well.

4 Add the stock or wine and stir-fry for 2–3 minutes until the beef is cooked through and the vegetables are tender-crisp. Serve immediately with rice noodles.

Beef & Bok Choy

A colourful selection of vegetables stir-fried with tender strips of steak.

SERVES 4

*1 large head of bok choy, about 250–275 g/ 8–9 oz, torn
into large pieces
2 tbsp vegetable oil
2 garlic cloves, crushed
500 g/ 1 lb rump or fillet steak,
cut into thin strips
150 g/ 5 oz mangetout (snow peas), trimmed
150 g/ 5 oz baby sweetcorn cobs
6 spring onions (scallions), chopped
2 red (bell) peppers, cored, deseeded and thinly sliced
2 tbsp oyster sauce
1 tbsp fish sauce
1 tbsp sugar
rice or noodles, to serve*

1 Steam the bok choy leaves over boiling water until just tender. Keep warm.

2 Heat the oil in a large, heavy-based frying pan (skillet) or wok, add the garlic and steak strips and stir-fry until just browned, about 1–2 minutes.

3 Add the mangetout (snow peas), baby sweetcorn cobs, spring onions (scallions), (bell) pepper, oyster sauce, fish sauce and sugar, mixing well. Stir-fry for 2–3 minutes until the vegetables are just tender, but still quite crisp to the bite.

4 Arrange the bok choy leaves in the base of a warmed serving dish and spoon the beef and vegetable mixture into the centre.

5 Serve the stir-fry immediately, with rice or noodles.

Green Beef Curry

This is a quickly-made curry of beef steak strips, cubed aubergine (eggplant) and onion in a cream sauce flavoured wth green curry paste. Serve with fluffy rice and a salad.

SERVES 4

1 aubergine (eggplant), peeled and cubed
2 onions, cut into thin wedges • 2 tbsp vegetable oil
Green Curry Paste (see page 26)
500 g/1 lb beef fillet, cut into thin strips
500 ml/16 fl oz/2 cups thick coconut milk or cream
2 tbsp fish sauce • 1 tbsp brown sugar
1 red chilli, deseeded and very finely chopped
1 green chilli, deseeded and very finely chopped
2.5 cm/1 inch piece of ginger root, finely chopped
4 kaffir lime leaves, torn into pieces
chopped fresh basil and lime wedges, to garnish
rice and green salad leaves, to serve

1 Blanch the aubergine (eggplant) cubes and onion wedges in boiling water for about 2 minutes, to soften. Drain thoroughly.

2 Heat the oil in a large heavy-based pan or wok, add the curry paste and cook for 1 minute.

3 Add the beef strips and stir-fry, over a high heat, for about 1 minute, to brown on all sides.

4 Add the coconut milk or cream, fish sauce and sugar to the pan and bring the mixture to the boil, stirring constantly.

5 Add the aubergine (eggplant) and onion, chillies, ginger and lime leaves. Cook for 2 minutes.

6 Transfer the curry to a warmed serving dish. Garnish with the basil leaves and lime wedges, and serve with rice and a green salad.

Fat Horses

This classic Thai snack is a great nibble for parties – but be sure to make plenty!

SERVES 4

30 g/ 1 oz/ 2 tbsp creamed coconut • 125 g/ 4 oz lean pork
125 g/ 4 oz chicken breast, skin removed
125 g/ 4 oz/ ½ cup canned crab meat, drained
2 eggs • 2 garlic cloves, crushed
4 spring onions (scallions), trimmed and chopped
1 tbsp fish sauce
1 tbsp chopped fresh coriander (cilantro) leaves and stems
1 tbsp dark muscovado sugar • salt and pepper

To garnish:
finely sliced white radish (mooli) or turnip • chives
red chilli • sprigs of fresh coriander (cilantro)

1 Put the coconut into a bowl and pour over 3 tablespoons of hot water. Stir to dissolve the coconut.

2 Put the pork, chicken and crab meat into a food processor or blender and process for 10–15 seconds until minced (ground), or chop them finely by hand and put in a mixing bowl. Add the coconut mixture to the food processor or blender with the eggs, garlic, spring onions (scallions), fish sauce, coriander (cilantro) and sugar. Season with salt and pepper and process for a few more seconds. Alternatively, mix these ingredients into the chopped meat.

3 Grease 6 ramekin dishes with a little butter. Spoon in the minced (ground) mixture, levelling the surface. Place them in a steamer, then set the steamer over a pan of gently boiling water. Cook until set – about 30 minutes. Lift out the dishes and leave to cool for a few minutes. Run a knife around the edge of each dish, then invert on to warmed plates to serve.

Green Rice

A deliciously different way to serve plain rice for a special occasion or to liven up a simple meal

SERVES 4

2 tbsp olive oil
500 g/ 1 lb/ 2¹/₄ cups basmati or Thai jasmine rice,
soaked for 1 hour, washed and drained
750 ml/ 1¹/₄ pints/ 3 cups coconut milk
1 tsp salt
1 bay leaf
2 tbsp chopped fresh coriander (cilantro)
2 tbsp chopped fresh mint
2 green chillies, deseeded and chopped finely
lime wedges, to garnish

1 Heat the oil in a saucepan, add the rice and stir until it becomes translucent.

2 Add the coconut milk, salt and bay leaf to the pan. Bring to the boil and cook until all the liquid is absorbed.

3 Lower the heat as much as possible, cover the saucepan tightly with the lid or a piece of foil and cook for 10 minutes. Remove the bay leaf.

4 Stir in the chopped coriander (cilantro), mint and green chillies. Fork through the rice gently and serve immediately, garnished with lime wedges.

Chatuchak Fried Rice

**An excellent way to use up leftover rice.
Pop it in the freezer as soon as it is cool,
and it will be ready to reheat at any time.**

SERVES 4

1 tbsp sunflower oil • *3 shallots, chopped finely*
2 garlic cloves, crushed
1 red chilli, deseeded and chopped finely
2.5 cm/1 inch piece of ginger root, shredded finely
½ green (bell) pepper, deseeded and sliced finely
150 g/5 oz/2–3 baby aubergines (eggplants), quartered
*90 g/3 oz sugar snap peas or mangetout
(snow peas), trimmed and blanched*
*90 g/3 oz/6 baby sweetcorn cobs, halved lengthways
and blanched*
1 tomato, cut into 8 pieces • *90 g/3 oz/1½ cups bean-sprouts*
500 g/1 lb/2¼ cups cooked Thai jasmine rice
2 tbsp tomato ketchup • *2 tbsp light soy sauce*
fresh coriander (cilantro) leaves and lime wedges, to garnish

1 Heat the oil in a wok or large, heavy frying pan (skillet) over a high heat. Add the shallots, garlic, chilli and ginger. Stir until the shallots have softened.

2 Add the green (bell) pepper and baby aubergines (eggplants) and stir. Add the sugar snap peas or mangetout (snow peas), baby sweetcorn, tomato and bean-sprouts. Stir for 3 minutes.

3 Add the rice, and lift and stir with 2 spoons for 4–5 minutes, until no more steam is released. Stir in the tomato ketchup and light soy sauce.

4 Serve immediately, garnished with coriander (cilantro) leaves and lime wedges to squeeze over the rice.

Massaman Curried Rice

Massaman paste is the mildest Thai curry paste, and makes a deliciously rich curry.

SERVES 4

Paste:

1 tsp coriander seeds • 1 tsp cumin seeds
1 tsp ground cinnamon • 1 tsp cloves • 1 whole star anise
1 tsp cardamom pods • 1 tsp white peppercorns
1 tbsp oil • 6 shallots, chopped very roughly
6 garlic cloves, chopped very roughly
5 cm/ 2 inch piece of lemon grass, sliced
4 fresh red chillies, deseeded and chopped
grated rind of 1 lime • 1 tsp salt
1 tbsp chopped roast peanuts to garnish

Curry:

3 tbsp sunflower oil
250 g/ 8 oz marinated tofu (bean curd),
cut into 2.5 cm/ 1 inch cubes
125 g/ 4 oz green beans, cut into 2.5cm/ 1 inch lengths
1 kg/ 2 lb/ 6 cups cooked rice (300 g/ 10 oz/ 1½ cups
raw weight)
3 shallots, diced finely and deep-fried
1 spring onion (scallion), chopped finely
2 tbsp chopped roast peanuts • 1 tbsp lime juice

1 To make the paste grind together the spices in a pestle and mortar or spice grinder. Heat the oil in a saucepan and add the shallots, garlic and lemon grass. Cook over a low heat for 5 minutes until soft, then add the chillies and grind with the dry spices. Stir in the lime rind and salt.

2 To make the curry, heat the oil in a wok or large, heavy frying pan (skillet). Cook the tofu (bean curd) over a high heat for 2 minutes to seal. Add the

paste and beans, and stir.
Add the cooked rice and,
using 2 spoons, lift and stir
over a high heat for about
3 minutes.

3 Transfer to a warmed
serving dish. Sprinkle with
the deep-fried shallots, spring
onions (scallions) and peanuts.
Sprinkle over the lime juice.

Paw-paw (Papaya) Salad

Choose firm paw-paws (papayas) for this delicious salad.

SERVES 4

Dressing:

4 tbsp olive oil • 1 tbsp fish sauce or light soy sauce
2 tbsp lime or lemon juice • 1 tbsp dark muscovado sugar
1 tsp finely chopped fresh red or green chilli

Salad:

1 crisp lettuce • ¼ small white cabbage
2 paw-paws (papayas) • 2 tomatoes
30 g/1 oz/¼ cup roast peanuts, chopped roughly
4 spring onions (scallions), trimmed and sliced thinly
basil leaves, to garnish

1 To make the dressing, whisk together the olive oil, fish sauce or soy sauce, lime or lemon juice, sugar and chopped chilli. Set aside, stirring occasionally to dissolve the sugar.

2 Shred the lettuce and cabbage and toss them together. Arrange on a large serving plate.

3 Peel the paw-paws (papayas) and slice them in half. Scoop out the seeds, then slice the flesh thinly. Arrange on top of the shredded lettuce and cabbage.

4 Put the tomatoes into a small bowl and cover them with boiling water. Leave them to stand for 1 minute, then lift them out with a fork and peel them. Remove the seeds and chop the flesh. Arrange them on the salad leaves. Scatter the peanuts and spring onions (scallions) over the top.

5 Whisk the salad dressing to distribute the ingredients and pour over the salad. Garnish with basil leaves and serve at once.